Editor
Eric Migliaccio

Managing Editor
Ina Massler Levin, M.A.

Illustrator
Vicki Frazier

Cover Artist
Barb Lorseyedi

Art Production Manager
Kevin Barnes

Imaging
Craig Gunnell

Publisher
Mary D. Smith, M.S. Ed.

GRADES K-2

APRIL
DAILY JOURNAL
WRITING PROMPTS

APR 1
APR 8
APR 15

Author

Maria Elvira Gallardo, M.A.

Teacher Created Resources, Inc.
6421 Industry Way
Westminster, CA 92683
www.teachercreated.com

ISBN: 978-1-4206-3133-3

©2005 Teacher Created Resources, Inc.
Reprinted, 2007
Made in U.S.A.

Table of Contents

Introduction

More than ever, it is important for students to practice writing on a daily basis. Every classroom teacher knows that the key to getting students excited about writing is introducing interesting topics that are fun to write about. *April Daily Journal Writing Prompts* provides kindergarten through second-grade teachers with an entire month of ready-to-use journal topics, including special holiday and seasonal topics for April. All journal topics are included in a calendar that can be easily reproduced for students. A student journal cover allows students to personalize their journal for the month.

Other useful pages that are fun include:

✛ **A Blank Calendar (pages 6 and 7)**

This can be used to meet your own classroom needs. You may want your students to come up with their own topics for the month, or it may come in handy for homework writing topics.

✛ **Word Banks (pages 40–43)**

These include commonly-used vocabulary words for school, holiday, and seasonal topics. A blank word bank gives students a place to write other words they have learned throughout the month.

✛ **April Author Birthdays (page 44)**

Celebrate famous authors' birthdays or introduce an author who is new to your students. This page includes the authors' birthdays and titles of some of their most popular books.

✛ **April Historic Events (page 45)**

In the format of a time line, this page is a great reference tool for students. They will love seeing amazing events that happened in April.

✛ **April Discoveries and Inventions (page 46)**

Kindle students' curiosity about discoveries and inventions with this page. This is perfect to use for your science and social-studies classes.

Motivate your students' writing by reproducing the pages in this book and making each student an individual journal. Use all the journal topics included, or pick and choose them as you please. See "Binding Ideas" on page 48 for ways to put it all together. Planning a month of writing will never be easier!

Monthly Calendar

A P R

1	2	3	4
A joke someone played on me was…	Bunny rabbits are…	If I went to the desert, I would see…	When I lose a tooth…
9	**10**	**11**	**12**
I'd like to become famous for…	I once stayed at a friend's house…	It's important to exercise because…	Someone I wish could be our substitute teacher is…
17	**18**	**19**	**20**
If I ever got lost…	If I could go back in time…	If I could build a robot…	An animal I know a lot about is…
25	**26**	**27**	**28**
If I were only one inch tall…	I want to take a field trip to…	When my parents go out, I stay with…	At the library I…

Monthly Calendar *(cont.)*

5 I use a computer for…	**6** My favorite P.E. activity is…	**7** I stay strong by eating…	**8** The biggest thing I've ever seen is…
13 That last time I cried was…	**14** My favorite assembly at school this year was…	**15** TV would be better if…	**16** The librarian at my school…
21 Roller coasters are…	**22** I help the Earth by…	**23** When I go to the dentist…	**24** A fun outdoor activity is…
29 Something that makes me feel good about myself is…	**30** I scream whenever I see…	**Special Topic** **Arbor Day** I want to plant a tree… **Spring** So far, spring has been …	

Blank Monthly Calendar

APR

1	2	3	4
9	10	11	12
17	18	19	20
25	26	27	28

Blank Monthly Calendar (cont.)

5	6	7	8
13	14	15	16
21	22	23	24
29	30		Free Choice Topics

A joke someone played on me was

_____

_____

_____

_____

_____

_____

_____

_____

Bunny rabbits are _____

_____

_____

_____

_____

_____

_____

_____

_____

_____

If I went to the desert, I would see

_____

_____

_____

_____

_____

_____

_____

_____

_____

_____

_____

When I lose a tooth _____

_____

_____

_____

_____

_____

_____

_____

_____

_____

_____

_____

I use a computer for _____

_____

_____

_____

_____

_____

_____

_____

_____

_____

_____

My favorite P.E. activity is _____

_____

_____

_____

_____

_____

_____

I stay strong by eating _____

_____

_____

_____

_____

_____

_____

_____

_____

_____

_____

_____

The biggest thing I've ever seen is

_____

_____

_____

_____

_____

_____

_____

_____

_____

_____

I'd like to become famous for _____

_____

_____

_____

_____

_____

_____

_____

_____

_____

I once stayed at a friend's house

_____

_____

_____

_____

_____

_____

It's important to exercise because

_____

_____

_____

_____

_____

_____

                                                   _____

                                                   _____

Someone I wish could be our substitute teacher is _____

_____

_____

_____

_____

_____

_____

_____

_____

_____

_____

The last time I cried was

My favorite assembly at school this
year was _____

_____

_____

_____

_____

_____

_____

_____

_____

_____

_____

_____

TV would be better if _____

_____

_____

_____

_____

_____

_____

_____

The librarian at my school _____

_____

_____

_____

_____

_____

_____

_____

_____

_____

_____

_____

If I ever got lost _____

_____

_____

_____

_____

_____

_____

_____

_____

_____

_____

Shoe World

If I could go back in time _____

_____

_____

_____

_____

_____

_____

_____

_____

_____

_____

_____

If I could build a robot _____

_____

_____

_____

_____

_____

_____

_____

_____

_____

_____

_____

An animal I know a lot about is _____

_____

_____

_____

_____

_____

_____

Roller coasters are _____

_____

_____

_____

_____

_____

_____

_____

_____

I help the Earth by _____

_____

_____

_____

_____

_____

_____

_____

_____

_____

_____

_____

When I go to the dentist _____

_____

_____

_____

_____

_____

_____

_____

_____

A fun outdoor activity is _____

_____

_____

_____

_____

_____

_____

_____

_____

If I were only one inch tall _____

_____

_____

_____

_____

_____

_____

_____

Fluffy

_____

_____

_____

I want to take a field trip to _____

_____

_____

_____

_____

_____

_____

_____

_____

_____

_____

When my parents go out, I stay with

_____

_____

_____

_____

_____

_____

_____

_____

34

At the library I _____

_____

_____

_____

_____

_____

_____

_____

Something that makes me feel good about myself is _____

_____

_____

_____

_____

_____

                                    _____

                                    _____

                                    _____

I scream whenever I see _____

_____

_____

_____

_____

_____

_____

_____

_____

_____

TOYS

I want to plant a tree _____

_____

_____

_____

_____

_____

_____

_____

_____

So far, spring has been _____

_____

_____

_____

_____

_____

_____

_____

_____

_____

_____

_____

School Word Bank

alphabet	desks	map	recess
art	dictionary	markers	report card
assembly	encyclopedia	math	rules
award	folder	notebook	science
binder	glue	office	scissors
board	grades	paper	stapler
books	history	pencils	study
bus	homework	pens	subject
children	journal	playground	teacher
class	learning	principal	thesaurus
crayons	lunch	reading	write

Holiday Word Bank

April Holidays

Arbor Day
Earth Day

National Library Week
World Health Day

appreciation	joke	recycle
birds	learn	reduce
books	leaves	resources
breakfast	librarian	reuse
city	litter	riddles
clean	lunch	rivers
community	nature	silly
conserve	neighborhood	stories
dinner	nutrition	study
environment	ocean	trash
exercise	planet	trees
foods	plant	trick
fool	pollution	United Nations
fun	prank	water
garden	protect	world
health care	public	
humor	read	

Seasonal Word Bank

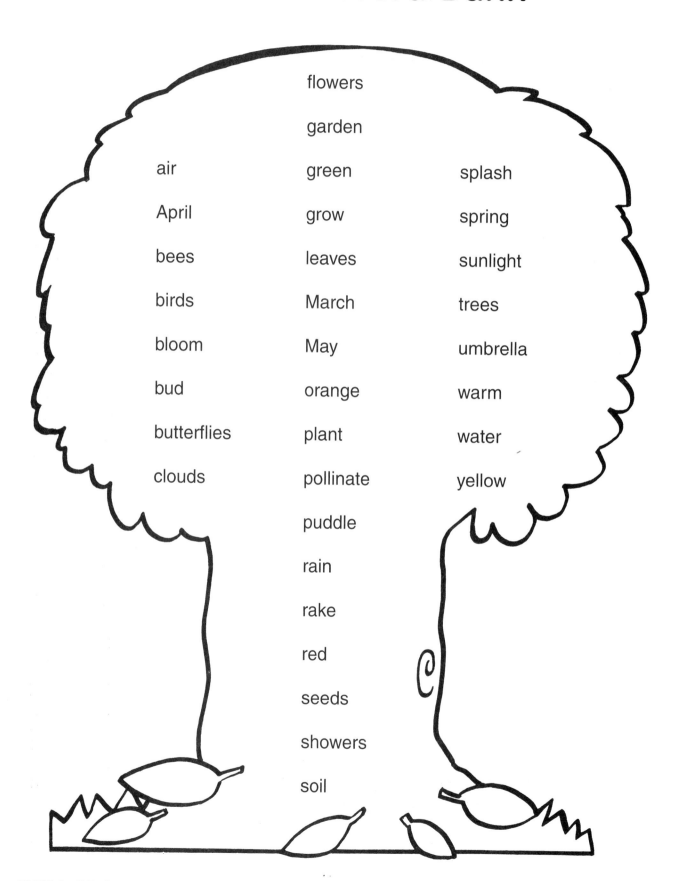

flowers

garden

air   green   splash

April   grow   spring

bees   leaves   sunlight

birds   March   trees

bloom   May   umbrella

bud   orange   warm

butterflies plant   water

clouds   pollinate yellow

puddle

rain

rake

red

seeds

showers

soil

My Word Bank

April Author Birthdays

1

Jan Wahl
(b. 1933)

Rabbits on Mars (Learner Publishing Group, 2003)

Knock! Knock! (Henry Holt and Co., 2004)

4

Glen Rounds
(b. 1906)

I Know an Old Lady Who Swallowed a Fly (Holiday House, 1990)

Once We Had a Horse (Holiday House, 1996)

4

Phoebe Gilman
(b. 1940)

Jillian Jiggs (Scholastic, 1985)

Grandma and the Pirates (Scholastic, 1990)

6

Graeme Base
(b. 1958)

Animalia (Harry N. Abrams, 1987)

The Water Hole (Harry N. Abrams, 2001)

8

Trina Schart Hyman
(b. 1939)

How Six Found Christmas (Holiday House, 1991)

The Alphabet Game (Seastar Books, 2000)

10

David Adler
(b. 1947)

Roman Numerals (HarperCollins, 1977)

Young Cam Jansen & the Zoo Note Mystery (Viking, 2003)

12

Hardie Gramatky
(1907–1979)

Sparky, the Story of a Little Trolley Car (Putnam, 1952)

Little Toot (Putnam, 1992)

12

Beverly Cleary
(b. 1916)

Two Dog Biscuits (William Morrow & Co., 1986)

The Real Hole (William Morrow & Co., 1986)

15

Jacqueline Briggs
(b. 1945)

Snowflake Bentley (Houghton Mifflin, 1998)

The Finest Horse in Town (Purple House Press, 2003)

21

Barbara Park
(b. 1947)

Junie B., First Grader (at last!) (Random House, 2001)

Psssst! It's Me…The Bogeyman (Atheneum, 1998)

26

Patricia Reilly Giff
(b. 1935)

Pickle Puss (Delcorte Books, 1986)

Look Out, Washington, D.C. (Yearling, 1995)

30

Dorothy H. Patent
(b. 1940)

Flashy, Fantastic Rain Forest Frogs (Walker & Co., 1999)

Slinky, Scaly, Slithery Snakes (Walker & Co., 2001)

April Historic Events

April 4, 1818
The U.S. Congress adopted the flag of the U.S. as having 13 red and white stripes and one star for each state, with additional stars to be added whenever a new state is added to the Union.

April 6, 1896
The first modern Olympic Games were held in Athens, Greece.

April 7, 1940
Booker T. Washington became the first African American to be depicted on a United States postage stamp.

April 9, 1833
The first public library in the U.S. opened in New Hampshire.

April 13, 1943
The Jefferson Memorial was dedicated in Washington, D.C., on the 200th anniversary of Thomas Jefferson's death.

April 15, 1955
The first McDonald's restaurant opened in Des Plaines, Illinois.

April 21, 1944
Women in France received the right to vote.

April 22, 1864
The U.S. Congress passed the Coinage Act, which mandated that the inscription "In God We Trust" be placed on all coins in the U.S.

April 24, 1990
The Hubble Space Telescope was launched by space shuttle *Discovery*.

April Discoveries and Inventions

1 **Apple Computer Company was formed** by Steve Jobs and Steve Wozniak in 1976.

3 **The first mobile phone call was placed** in 1973 by Martin Cooper in New York City.

7 **The friction match was invented** in 1827 by John Walker, an English chemist.

9 **Robert de LaSalle discovered the mouth of the Mississippi River** in 1682. He claimed it for France and named it Louisiana.

The first edition of *Webster's Dictionary* was copyrighted by Noah Webster in 1828.

14 **Thomas Edison demonstrated the kinetoscope** on this day in 1894. This device could show photographs that flipped in sequence, a precursor to movies.

19 **Australia was first spotted** by Captain James Cook in 1770.

20 **The first pasteurization test was completed** in 1862 by Louis Pasteur and Claude Bernard.

21 **In 1994, astronomer Alexander Wolszczan discovered evidence of extrasolar planets**—planets which orbit a star other than the sun and therefore belong to a planetary system other than our solar system.

22 **Brazil was first sighted** by the Portuguese navigator Pedro Alvares Cabral in 1500.

30 **The ice-cream cone made its debut** in 1904.

April
Journal

by

_____

Binding Ideas

Students will be so delighted when they see a month of their writing come together with one of the following binding ideas. You may choose to bind their journals at the beginning or end of the month, once they have already filled all of the journal topic pages. When ready to bind students' journals, have them color in their journal covers on page 47. It may be a good idea to reproduce the journal covers on hard stock paper in order to better protect the pages in the journal. Use the same hard stock paper for the back cover.

Simple Book Binding

1. Put all pages in order and staple together along the left margin.

2. Cut book-binding tape to the exact length of the book.

3. Run the center line of tape along the left side of the book and fold to cover the front left margin and the back right margin. Your book is complete!

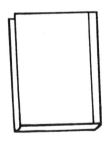

Yarn-Sewn Binding

1. Put all pages in order and hole-punch the left margin.

2. Stitch the pages together with thick yarn or ribbon.